On *Time Being*:

Charles Alexander's *Time Being* looks into the ordinary moment
to find a site of revealing beyond time. Subtle rhythm divides
its alert listening somewhere between Coltrane and walking; it
listens in on the ways of space through the active body's own
prosody: "don't count, don't/use measure in that way/step step
and turn in/the only dance that might/turn again." It gives
a sense of *instant poem* that instructs in its own sensory time
being—toward the unpredictable point of verbal satori.

Series like "Th'expense of spirit," with its torsional syntax,
enact a process of *thinking onward* with particular ontological
force, like seeing the mind changing as it speaks, then feeding
on the energy stirred up. It works in a compositional process
that *knows out loud,* by way of a self-guiding syntax of further
being. Its song tunes in to where excitable mind finds soul in
the telling. Along the way it replays certain Elizabethan musics
living on now where we can hear them—still telling tales we
didn't know we *need* to hear.

— George Quasha
   Artist, poet, and musician working
   across mediums to explore principles
   in common within language, sculpture,
   drawing, video, sound, installation, and
   performance.

time being

time being

(some incidents)

Charles Alexander

CHAX PRESS 2023

Cover painting by Cynthia Miller:
House and Garden, ©2023 Cynthia Miller

ISBN 978-1-946104-48-9

LIBRARY OF CONGRESS CONTROL NUMBER: 2023946748

Chax Press books are supported in part by individual donors and
by sales of books. Please visit *https://chax.org/membership-support/* if
you would like to contribute to our mission to make an impact on
the literature and culture of our time. Chax books have also been
supported by the Arizona Commission on the Arts and the Arts
Foundation for Tucson and Southern Arizona.

We thank our current assistants, Ben Leitner and Erika Cruz, for
their work on Chax book projects. Our Art Director, Cynthia Miller,
contributes to all books Chax publishes.

chax press
6181 east fourth street
tucson arizona 85711
usa

chax.org

for Cynthia

here and everywhere

Contents

An incident here and there,
and rails gone (for guns)
from your (and my) old town square;

— H.D., *The Walls Do Not Fall*

But where are the bounds of the incidental?

What is your aim in philosophy? — *To shew the fly the way out of the fly-bottle.*

How could this seem ludicrous? It is, as it were, a dream of our language.

My aim is: to teach you to pass from a piece of disguised nonsense to something that is patent nonsense.

((A multitude of paths lead off from these words in every direction.))

((Meaning is a physiognomy.))

— Ludwig Wittgenstein,
Philosophical Investigations
(translated by G.E. Anscombe)

Precipitation Meditation

precipitation   meditation
           thunderous
                    exclamation

the denial of
dimension is
           another
           dimension

forgetting the frog
forgetting the pond
wet
wet

thundering herds
effervescent thirds
Beethoven
and Bach
           on a picnic

Mingus   sing us
a fauvian burst
of the lowest chord
a roasted gourd
eliminating thirst
or again in spring   bring us

agora and agony
antigone revives
              the sun

what's new my cat?
              what mews is this
              on thunder sits?
hawk cries in the rain

hedgerows hardly hedgerows
harrows hardly fair, and air
cuts through the trees toward
the hedgerows
hardly

random is not a
      random word
      or a possible chance
      on chance
      a justice inscribed

find the bird was a game
mind the word is a game
a mindless world seems
      possibly not a game

what rushes in
what rushes out
a math problem

shall we shake
up some atoms today

      not explosion only
        breathing

in the air she twists she
      defies everything
      but the imaginary
  and in the mind
      twists and may
      be defied

intention of   attention

      oh blarney
      nine javelina are
      just outside the window

neoliberalism may be
      a dead horse but
      its foal are manifest
         mean and
         meandering

the top of the pot has blown off
      to release a searing steam
      uncaring   unfettered

love is perhaps like
hair follicles
        in short supply when
        any filter between the
        ever-hotter sun and the
        collective dome of our head
        would be welcome

        the brain boils in
        absence of that quality

        fox in its hole
        cat in its box
        priest in his closet
        we in our zoombox
        god in his heaven
        all's right with the world   (hang it all)

Plutarch
is an oligarch
on Noah's ark
now in Central Park

Horace
doesn't bore us
and Ovid
can't catch covid

Browning
may be frowning
while So-shu is drowning
Inanna comes crowning

We read at random the world
          as our disease
          because it is
                    and our dis-ease
                    because we are

Haiku 2022

January

we feed each other
first the cats, then the birds
    squirrels, come out too!

money out, money in
    must be winter, but snow
        does not fall here

money out, money in
    must be autumn
        the leaves fall around

sake or whiskey
choices of color
    the moon lies close tonight

zazen in process
    the cat asks two times
    to come in, come in

cats or machines
which will last longer
        a paw finds the off button

        afar and away I have
                written before but only
walked part way over

over hill over dale
        the ravaged western
place of speed and missiles

occident and orient
all the way to the
global capital spittoon

        water on the ground
she says, amazed by
moist desert no mirage

january is the coolest
        month of sweaters
        lit by sunlight

another birthday or two
      or three and perhaps
            that's enough

he said he had forgotten
more than I will know
            and now I know

tree trimmed now
the ground has risen
mulch elevation high

friday and the hot
baked pizza has not
        yet risen

for most of a tree
        climbing life I
        loved the limbs

the birds come for
        seeds and each
                other's company

the company of poets
        no words needed
        today

some words have not yet
been found and we suffer
alone and in the language
free the wandering syllable
        frozen thought
        forgotten solution

twentyone days gone
        this month or any
way I turn

two aleppo pines
        reach the sky, the heart pines
                then leaps to the limbs

snow and ice, the hurt
        pain and loss, or
        illusion

roseate spoonbill on
the long sand beach
              a brief moment

pitchfork barn and knee
with bleeding hole
a scar, I remember

zazen is one and
other and not two
and not one today

         Wudang in rain
the grey, the green, the grand
           loss of all things

cold with no language
          shared, no problem
we eat and warm together

seventeen water drops
        hang from eaves, a wet
               haiku ready to fall

      not today the sixteen
      or less or more upon
blank screens everywhere

      what happens when
      winter sun has no snow
             to melt, noone to warm

February

we are the battered
      who   the undone
      and   what remains

February in a bloom blaze
      of petals   white stars
      early cold morning

and Venus a train
      so light and fast I
wait at the station

what we arrange we
      derange or disarrange
      clouds over Catalinas

bronze age warmer
      than today but ice is
            a threnody of tones

on the street I ask for
      Naima and he cries, says
      it is his favorite song

around the bend of
      the Guadalupe lies
another bend   the way

hedgerows may hardly
be hedgerows but rows
and rows and rows

seven candles
in the fireplace
through the night

blood from the cut
knuckle wound but
no mosquito near

tied in a knot that
disippates with tea
and sitting

tied in a knot that
stays a knot, today
is not the day

an equal sign but
what is on
the left and the right

no sign no guide no light
but there (or here)
no corridor   just a field

      a love supreme
        no more no less
hawks nest in the aleppo trees

      a love supreme
        no less no more
seals play in the waves

how far can the
        saxophone go, oh
         notes gone now

whither and wither and
        when it wanes
        the rain falls

rain falls again in
        a desert town
no line   no time

$1 \div 1$
does not speak well
of the mathematics of wall

virus a season word
all through the year
        and then again

        again the hawks
carry sticks and leaves
        to the high branches

four small javelina
        colliding fur specks
        on a small planet

incendiary words
or letters or
maybe just phonemes

who says words do not
burn, have you seen
the red world, read world

not a bang yes a bang
and an electric band
      along a former wall

      maybe and maybe
      and maybe not but
      who gets to decide

March

a paper document allows
      one to cross a line
            or receive a meal

so much language
      every day and
      now, a single word

a single word sings
      in wings in wind
      finds flight

why do you think
       speech happens, because
       we can, you can

a word a wind a wood
       all permeable like
       the water, the life

a poet restores
       the language that's what
       I heard today

I heard today a word
       and pray a bird
       and birth occurred

afternoon of light
through windows words
in the gusty air

check your battery
will you please but
don't back up

reverse the engines
verse invites the errant winds
behind the sails

Batman to Cups

Batman walks Dr. Seuss into Symphony Hall.
Dvorzak's 9th is playing, and the room is filled with people
who don't know who they are. That is, each one is either a lost
soul, or, at least, can't decide on a major. The Kindergarten
Song plays at intermission. "What thou lovest well remains"
is a refrain for old men. "Keep it hot" may be today's hit song,
but will it last? A nurse in the third row leaves a bare branch in
her seat as she leaves for the refrain of bright city lights. Frodo
follows her, carrying a ring that he wishes to place on the finger
of Elizabeth Bennett, before they embark on a honeymoon
to Japan, where they will drink tea from pentatonically toned
cups.

for now   *(for david)*

      proputty

      proputty

      proputty

              pivoted

              pivoted

              pivoted

      vaccin
      ate

the square root of 19 equals zero

proputty pivoted / canter away

        (*when did you make the connection between*
             bloated bodies and bloated economies? (roy miki)

As If

I think as if
    or if I think

      might
      could
      would

it be better simply
where you will be

      tomorrow
      and if we did
      and could touch

so much
for an afternoon

*

"Music avoids impossibility."

says Z
in the key
of C

so much for the possible
      inconsistency a beauty

*

for age an adjustment
forage widely one

thirsts another feels
wet everywhere

    and an eye to see it
    or see where it
    leads

      (it leads)

let it go let
them go let
the world in

    more than a
    word at a
    time

*

    (I find you
    here today I
    am glad you
    found the way
    here, found me
    too, today)

*

just as the whole world is made up of many people, each idea contributes to its whole sense, even if it appears only as its dark shadow—Friedrich Schleiermacher

*

just so, the world
　　　as it fills and
　　　falls, from the
　　　center, the
　　　inclination shadows
　　　and foreshadows

between written and
spoken, a function
to inhabit

no other difference remains
no other no
remains or the
fact stands with
and beyond the light

*

whole lemon light

　　　I once wrote, young
　　　and warm, the
　　　page warm as
　　　an evening

and in the morning
now, the light out
shines lemon, fruit
of all kind, years
of one duration
or another

*

when you or I
write a word,
all the previous
words occasion
the possibility,
and what we do
changes the nature
of such future
occasions, as well
as the nature of
the current

*

the mouth blesses
its space, or
the space around

you have moved in
such spaces and we
have known you

moving on walls on
walks inside small
and large spaces

sometimes with giant
steps and love su-
preme love of the air

that parts to let you
through let you in
let you go it

is hard going from here
for those who let
you go   we do

and bless your
space with our
mouth, our moving

*

a compassion to
yours a line of
worry and care
a pomegranate a
butterfly a few
words on paper

limbo   bats   coffee   (haiku)

sitting in limbo
do bats have buddha nature?
drink your coffee now

two coffee haiku

sit in the dark cup
brewing up, emerging whole
in white porcelain

coffee clatch with a
kolache while listening
to The Clash, *calling*

bats

baseball bats Jackie
Robinson and Henry
Aaron   I remember
their beauty

Th' expense of spirit in a waste of shame

Don't do it, don't blast the window or shake the timbers,
     no, the whirlwind is quite enough, and when it
happens,
     where ever it happens, there will be bodily fluids
  including
tears and no small sense of regret.
                   Shake it all, shake it
all down, the statues, the bronze horses, the flies buzzing
in the summer of our undoing, in the future of our doing.

Is lust in action; and till action, lust

Oh so you sing, so you shake hips and swerve upon tides
even in the desert where mountains burn and streets become
sites of bodies moving forward, lithely and clumsily,
    no help from the authorities, their clubs and pepper gas
shall turn into colorful wings upon the wind, and we in
each other's presence shall shed a skin and find action,
        action, our blood our minds our furthest flights.

Is perjured, murd'rous, bloody, full of blame,

          oh Mr. Adams, I say, did you really believe the local
bank would be your friend, the federal purpose waning
      in the wake of bodies in streets, bodies under knees,
      you sousa-prophetic maniac of the 18th century, how did
      you think it might go, where did you want to take us
if your dream had not been hijacked by the wealth of nations.

Savage, extreme, rude, cruel, not to trust,

Turn it around,   turn it toward   those who
    lift a hand to
bloody a throat,   who lift a knee   to
    stomp a breath, but
listen to the hawk   with his sharp and uneven call,
        her
        fierce flight and cry to save her hawklet who takes a
        first flight toward freedom, extreme yes but necessary,
a way to trust again beyond any cruel false and impotent
    wisdom.

Enjoyed no sooner but despisèd straight,

for this is not a sonnet, nor any semblance thereof,
ragged and bony are we, flesh and that which would
strike the flesh, come on, scream now and find your
own bluesing
              fly with me
              all right, hawks and
              friends upon
              the burning mountain.

Past reason hunted; and, no sooner had

we turned another cheek than we lost all the flesh on
all our cheeks and began wandering again. What will
we find? Where will we go?

                don't count, don't
                use measure in that way
                step step and turn in
                the only dance that might
                turn again.

Past reason hated as a swallowed bait

What swallows from the throat, what swallows air, what
swallows its tail, what
turns
    cartwheels on rocks.

On purpose laid to make the taker mad;

When mad I had a hat, when off the hat I had a dream,
where a large hand lifted up and showed that everything
might be in air aloft, that every thing could be just one thing
but then he woke, then you woke, then I woke,
and where were we, on the other side of who's world?

Mad in pursuit and in possession so,

We are possessed, our possessions possess us, go
buy and by, and go by the night, go by the day,
go in flight, over the fray, over the once softly
held night flesh, mad mad mad, so that:
               this and that for which
               in term in time no time
               insane not in vain pull
               that down you lovers
               in pure chase in pure
               abandon all ye.

Had, having, and in quest to have, extreme;

Determined,
            dared,
                       done
is the tattoo I wish for, the one not painful but
extreme in its shimmering, a quest had better
have and have and had a worthy goal but not
an end, do not end, now or in any determined
sense of a way to find, a finding out, an out out out.

A bliss in proof and proved, a very woe;

poof poof fool whorl whipporwill will whisk
or find some food to fill the hole, fill the bowl,
fill the whole, oh woe oh whoa
                              this is not the end
                              this is not the beginning
                    these are not trifles or poofs
                    but proofs verily verily
                              to a theorem therein therefrom thereby.

Before, a joy proposed; behind, a dream.

A proposition, Joe, a sentence, a moment, and that
contains what comes before, what moved behind
and what is foretold, a proposal a marriage an epithalamion
upon the burning slope of the mountain, within the rocks
within the juniper and piñon,

> gather me
> gather us
> propose the sentence (the dance).

All this the world well knows; yet none knows well

what is a world, what is none
   until we pause and sit under a tone
         beside a stone within astonished thunder
         that is silent and unheard within our own
         meditations, not until we pause there will
         we know what is not known, know well
         what might be another word.

To shun the heaven that leads men to this hell.

                                      Aye,
                              there's the rub
    and you can rub all you want, with hot touch undress
cold water
        the methods of this madness shun sense
        and take the wrong step, the wrong lining
        to the current wrap, the place in which we find
        ourselves, the pacing with which we might surprise
        the commonwealth under a shunned stone.

Source: Willliam Shakespeare. Sonnet 129.

SHALL I then silent be or shall I speake?

Who's talking, and why, and with all that's happening,
how dare anyone suggest silence, unless on this road
lies the preservation of life, for another occasion,
another memorial, another poem, another day.

> Day of word
> day of silence
> shall you speak?

And if I speake, her wrath renew I shall:

Speech engenders anger
       anger begets blood
              wrath may sit alone on a throne

or will we be the phoenix, arise from flame
       and speak, speak, now and ever

and if I silent be, my hart will breake,

        haven't we heard this before
        haven't all hearts broken
        break the pipe / break the stone
        with the deer we run, whoso list
                hearts and hinds
                darts to minds

or choked be with ouerflowing gall.

      choked
      yoked
      oak
            fall the wall the everwall
      broken we must stand
      fallen we must fly

      my overflow shall not be blood
      my guilt shall not be soaked

      gall
      fall (not)
      call

What tyranny is this both my hart to thrall,

shall I then / follow when
alas and away / a word and a dream
a prison a wall in thrall and both
parties fail to find
       the water washes over
       the water washes under
       the water washes away

and eke my toung with proud restraint to tie?

ache each taste
each poison tongue taste
each unlit flame burn
what place restraint, what place pride
what tide ties us all
what tongue speaks

that nether I may speake nor thinke at all,

     be quiet be near be afraid be a feather
         be a thought
         trapped in a choke crushed with a knee
     be you or be I or nether underneath the ground
     below the world below
     the circles below the middle of our years
     be, just be, do not think, do not speak, not now

but like a stupid stock in silence die.

       stupid is as stupid does
       stupid fuck on the street in the fields
       stupid what silences
       stupid what kills
       stupid what defers a dream
       oh stupid your time has come and gone
       gone gone puff puff of smoke of ash of fire

Yet I my hart with silence secretly

forlorn, the poet's word, the word that echoes through
silence, resounds in silence, and all the deer in the forest
flee, and choose not to put themselves in danger,
        but seek change, seek it now, seek it in a street that
               has laid bodies down, no it was no dream
                  and we live in the knowledge
                  we die in the knowledge
                  we live again (when) (when) (when)

will teach to speak, and my iust cause to plead:

        teach me song
               teach me love
                      teach me more
     I would I were open to it
     I would you were open to it
     I would it were open to us
     just a plea doesn't work
             but a honk a squeal as trane
             as meditations as ascension
             as the hole at the end of the fall
                        go through go far go justly
             (it was just a dream some of us had)

and eke mine eies with meeke humility,

mine eyes have not seen the glory
        mine eyes have not shone with glory
if love is to reason as eyes to mind, what are
            knees to necks
            ropes hanging from trees
                  some have had humility far too long
                  some do not know that word
 my meek eyes
my humble eyes

            not long now, not long

loue learned letters to her eyes to read.

love is a game
love is a goat
love is a goal
love wanders and sheds light where it goes

let her have letters, let her say what she sees
read the book don't buy the coat
read the book (read it again)

Which her deep wit, that true harts thought can spel,

which witch? wit who? which who? with wit
a true heart melts
a heart through thought consults
with wit / spells the scene
casts a spell within which

we spin
salve salvage

wil soone conceiue, and learne to construe well.

a child is given to us
a soon child a son a daughter
we conceive concepts
a child is a concept
a concept is a construction
a construction is to be learned
a child conceives and learns a concept
soon a child soon a concept soon
       well, say you
       well met
       well joined
       inkwell
       deep well of cool water

Source: SONNET. XLIII. Edmund Spenser. Amoretti.

May the Dumplings

"May I eat the dumplings on the stove?"
You may,
you may eat the dumplings
on the stove
or in any nook
or cranny
you may,
you may eat the dumplings.

When did you make the dumplings
on the stove? I made them at the
edge of morning, after the birds
had been fed, before I left the house,
to buy wine for the weekend, I
made the dumplings for lunch,
and left some on the stove for you.

You have eaten those dumplings.
I am pleased you have eaten the dumplings.
I went away and returned with wine
and noticed right away that the dumplings
were gone except for one remaining on
the plate with the dipping sauce. You may
also eat the last dumpling. You have, you
have eaten the last dumpling.

love you in a place where there's no space or time (L. Russell)

a gate always open

for love is

between and the

sky knows

how does the sky know?

between

points uncharted

and everything that is not the case

she lies with the grass and dirt she lies with the stars

he lies with the grass and dirt he lies with the stars

we remain enclosed

among

to dwell is to live among

love might be a voice in a rain

    rain down wind and rain down

        one hears a note and a drop and feels

wet, everywhere wet, but still speaking

    amid the shower

        shower and share a sound

not quite a voice but a sound we live with

        in the between dwell and speak space

we call "ours" as though we have a claim

        on what we share, on each other's time

and skin a body hearing a note becoming

        wet in a rain one walks among

          and between and listens

            to voices in the rain

on the body on the skin mid day's music

Patientia

patience a gossamer thread inside
a go somewhere head, perhaps
the filaments of selves and senses
displayed over time, then seen
to fill years and spaces, no hurry
needed, no needless seeking after
logic and conclusion, nothing a
spider could not find inside herself

inside her capably negative form
of decision, form of instinctual
pattern, stunning in its disinterest
in anything but the arc of being
in silence and slow time slow
time turning as the dancer did
not race but floated across the
stage of memory, days and years

Surrounding the Darkened Disc of the Moon

every pattern has a chaos
                    (virus)
and chaos has a plan
                    (virus)
regular like ticking until
a tree falls through the
  (virus)
wall and into our life
                    (virus)

the morphology is the chorology
of virus known in all its
forms, expanded into field
whereupon *we* understand *us*
as part of the geography
part of the governed
this chaos that plan
one tree or many our life
a contagion of propositions

(here the notebook contains two blank pages as if nothing
came today, no one in the stands, no one on the bus,
a trace only a scent a passing of a microbe perhaps

indistinguishable to the eye ear nose or a slap in the heart
getting dark too dark to see

when ache genders a gap
(there is no gap   no gender)
equal compliance equal contagion
no poet smoothing the edge
no un-Stein or un-infection
curious this queering occurs
in the flower the lack
refolded over a species a
population a security and
we/us imagine a conduct counter
to the spread to the management

(this is the work from the blue notebook)

when it comes will it want
a variation on a theme or step
in an improvisational pedagogy
moving to an unkempt teaching
an unkempt body politic an
unkept keeping stranger than
a nuclear pause a place to view

if we fence away madness where
do I go inside the image a language
finds its way to desire
                (virus)
beside it next to it within it inside it
far from it no worship of it around
it over it under it off of it as
it goes beside it self
                (virus)
as it sees it
done with it
done with it
done with it

a truth a path on the continents
the plural words one after another
            (virus)
toward a center no frame no
time no words
        (no virus)
decay or just what happens
(dancing)

once a water on stone and the
stone stood up saying I am a fable
                 (virus)

and you are the written
                    (virus)
tell me when/where to open
                              (virus)
tell you where/when to close
                              (no virus)

and the words in rows
are the world's eros and
          turn and
          turn and
          turn and

          (the circle that is interrupted)

Thoughts in Air

I do not say X is better
I say, *to me,* X is better,
one poet or another,
a poet or a leaf

but *better* — what is
better, is as butter
does, melts as
we know what we
know

The world is
wet with things and
we lose them, one
by one

To reconcile
possibly means to
come again to the
isle, I'll find out
at another time when

I come to be
there or just come
to be, as Olson said,
"we are what we come to be"

The sea, there, all *theres*
at once, directions they are,
surrounds the isle, all the other isles

I will

19 February 2020 written while in air between Tucson &
Dallas/Forth Worth

Today and When

old sexton keeps the key to, the old

today and when I say is when

or if when then perhaps not or

take it from me if you can take

another joke or jump the hedge

service as rare as frost as privileged

the fly has flown for that is what

flies do or overdue by end of week

if time can take or be taken up

by those whose flaps are flipped

to left or right upon the shelf the

as cotton twill though linen thread

swerves better into the spines of books

today and when you say it may be

done the oven will open the door

will close and who enters from

the storm who enters to the story

when story has been missed as an

uncertain opportunity so hold on hold

onto the ring the train has stopped

and started on the way uptown on

the way to where we listen to what we

have heard or the third turn to the left

Written to Music

which way is silent or which way is which
which which or not or the space in the room
the space in the room may not be contained by the room
the room space which could or could not map the room space
open the door and let light in open the light and
let yourself in open the room and the space in
the room turns blue does it turn blue or is that
even a turn a turn u turn blue turn you turn
someone or some radio on and there it is or
their radio is set on the channel that channels
time and time may or may not be a silent way
just ask the question what question the question
that appears in blue light in the middle of your
room your space your face who are the
people here can we trust them can we put hats on
them and ask them to dance in the room to a
music they can only hear when they place a barrier
between themselves and others between
themselves and the sound of their own bodies have
you ever folded an ear over and suddenly
heard the sound of your pulse quicker than you
might imagine slower than a death march
here sounds the sound of a not very silent way
for we do not march with silence we do
not silence our marchers we do not murder

our citizens never today on the street or even
in an unexpurgated public speech for
silence will find us all it is the rest and
the rest is silence but is that a way or is it
a wall a wall between here and there where
here is our current habitation and there is
some space we'd like to be where we could
live where we could save ourselves save something
of ourselves each one each two each bit of connective
tissue before we devour such spaces before the rest
really is a silence we can't penetrate because we
have nothing left no room no pulse no breath no

blow   and
         blow

love
     further
     the green synapse
         the white silence

     the black notes upon a square

         don't interpret this as a picture
         don't hear this as a sound

         and blow
         and blow

forget the night
     before it leaves
     moon do you hear me

         moon do you hear me
         or have you shut yourself down
            for an evening's nap

moon can I hear you
     or have I closed my two ears
        to bask in your light

         moon oh moon oh light
      if you want me I am here
           with no resistance

can you read by moon
   light or can you read moon light
     in its own language

        can the moon read now
          that all the books have
been closed

    and what words will dance

moon or no moon or
    just the shadow in its light
       walking round and round

Dream logic questions nights
　　　　and trees an journeys
　　　　can go anywhere -- stay safe
　　　　　　day & night

Mom and dad, oh super ones
　　　　never lost never bled away
　　　　as justice may intervene

western cowboy or girl
in the light　　　　the moon
　　　　laughs and clouds over

could be Dionysus
　　or just a fellow in
　　a red jacket holding a glass

haiku for tenors
　　whose circumscribed notes foretell
　　　　a common day's loss

but where is the noise
　　　　the truck and the explosion
　　　　only color ever

nothing condenses
nothing considers alternatives

nothing bends

      sun comes in blue cloud spaces
      cloud fails to inhibit air
      goes out to our farthest dreams

      do not remove anything when
      you love   enjoy acres
      and glances to and
      fro

      farther away frightened
      away   fathered   away
      frittered away alas
      and away as far
      as   a stringed sound
      takes you today   or
      another day

      and then I woke up
      to a strung note held
      in a cloud's arc
      and then we anced

nowhere is a place
on a map   an unknown
topic of demarcation

full of hands full
of fingers full of
hairs full of face
full of conjunction
and connection full
of holes in the middle
of letters full of
mind full of air

who was John Dowland
when did he live
what inspired him to write
such beautiful notes expanding
the breath we need

la mer	mercy lo
la mer	abandon hope
la mer	dive and go
la mer	a man I know
la mer	to be yes oh

for the sea is our being

for the sea is our end

to see what there is to sea

to sea what there is to see

above   and below   or standing widdershins

beyond first waves   the seals
swim through the crests
and we can or can not
accompany the breaking

from debussy to davis
we hear the not so silent sea
the C of minor impact
the cool C of a baritone saxophone
the tristanic sea of melancholy
the miles and miles of sea and C
and is that you and is that me
he answered to her as the
ocean, from the ocean, to Cynthia
the name she shared with the moon
the light she borrowed from the sun
oh love can we be at the ocean
edge again walking into water

The World is a Book

The world is a book. I haven't read it all.
No one has read it all. It's not digital, and
it's not available on audio. It is, however,
present in a forest, in a place called
Dogtown or Nokomis, and it hasn't been
shot down yet or had the breath taken
out of it. It's sewn, not stapled or perfect
bound. It's sewn, and the thread is
archival, permanent. We're in that book,
you and you and I. You can't stop reading
it. If you do, you must take the bookmark
out, and start again from the beginning
when you pick it up. You might be able to
go to sleep under it, and read it by some
kind of osmosis understood by poets
and bookmakers everywhere because of
their training or proclivities. In the book
is the only time you get to have a mind, a
mind is a precious thing, no, really, eggs in
a skillet or book on a shelf. The book is
on the shelf, but I'm about to take it
down and open it.

Lifting Wing

with thanks to Lynda Zwinger

lift a wing sing
little singer ring ring
a pun spun upon
a word run among
little hawk squawk
ma and pa roar aaagh
in the leaves left
or the lives bereft
of rules and regul-
ation's formation
lift eye to hued sky
in a post-rain frame
the summons upon us
fly now or try resist
gravity does not insist
sun's blast not yet cast
in extreme heat defeat
before autumn plummet
toward some downward
prophet's words profit's
motive exploding
while iceberg eroding
ocean unfolding motion

to star alas afar

in a water order

or a broader motor

far flung field flame

to rename and untame

reframe unshame

and unalign the sine

and the cosine sign

shine 'til almost blind

spot and shot and not

singularly syllabary

minded unwinded

unearthed and birthed

forth was the firth

the free the freeze

breeze over seas

siesta unless disaster

raster and vector

master and rector

sequester not fester

unless your wrist

remainders the danger

now anger reminds

caterwauling behind
a cat or a wall no mind
becomes a moment
without some torment
fortune's mortuary
if the slip slips the fall
falls the mind unminds
the triptych in thirds
replays the open chords
refrays the harmolodic
fracture the unforeseen
conjunction the wind's
wing lifted and sifted
but fast and waste not
safe and sound found
outside the compound
inside the insight
among the Hmong or
furrowing the forwards
frown not brown cow
not brown milk or mown
grass of course an ass
is a sassy lad and asks

forgiveness only badly
on a Wednesday wind
and wing a word home
bring a girl a phone
make a promise rose
and rise a surprise on
a day of rest a stay
of circumstance and
confusion momentary
or monumental night's
fight for lasting sight
where what lasts or loves
well remains in reach
not preach or beach
towel trowel to vowel
a and e amen to she
and her seaman free man
in Paris where the ferris
wheel across the channel
churns the sea so
shoes wave up and save
their laces for traces
and faces in the crowd

aloud for sake's aloud
and shake a sound
astounding right in
the river bend the sliver
run the shiver snow
beguiles the child for
just an hour not with
power but powder but
not louder no shouting
lifting wing just swing
lifting sing a high song
strong wing soar upon
pun sprung and spun long

the last of the pushing waters

the last of the pushing waters

            until
                    it's not the last because
        doctor says so, says
                    there are no
                            perfect waves
        though we have lived
                    our lives   by water
                    by wits
                    or by accident
                            yes by

accident or wave and perhaps
there are no accidents either

                    either / or and the space between

we have lived

       our lives   by water
whether the deep blue
       of the Pacific with   its mighty
       lives of whales
          and waves and survivors
       Ishmael among
          others
       Ishmael among   the letters and numbers

       or rivers mostly dry and mostly
       sandy   the Rillito   the San Juan

and the Canadian the longest
       tributary
          of the Arkansas, begins
       in Colorado and at various points
       sand pits along the banks witness
          acts of love and the migrations
             of birds, such as cranes

       cranes move in waves

and we live by water, a few creeks or washes
      wet or dry because we find ourselves
both wet and dry in and out of rains in
and out of other sorts of tears

    here the poem washes up
    and washes us because
        without the poem we have
          steady drips but no
pools no lives that speak of Life we could
not live with (I cannot live with you) nor live without

now the waters in the canyon recede

    but the blooms are full on full on
        in orange and white and purple and
    pink and red
    colors of canyons
    colors of love's imaginings, no no hope
      if not a coral island
        slowly forming

      out there
      among the waves
    the crash   of the waves

among
of
blue
crest
old and new
bright reflection
broken with
branches and time
come home how
white and erect
sweet it
may
again and again

start again with accident
    and apology
        once upon a leaf who
        was there when I placed
            the leaf upon
            a doorway a leaf
        inscribed with words
        on an autumn day
            in California's cool east bay

for a friend to find
a poem to find and love
      to find a way make all
      things find a way

     a way and a wing and a wave
        gather and disperse

the last of the pushing
the last of the falling
      waters gather and disperse
      in warm April in the years not
         quite beyond
              disease or desire
              disperse and gather
              desire and contract
                now release

she flies
she flies again
a small hawk waits
for her return

     and across
     waters and lands and waters
     time wisdom and koalas wait
     for other returns other time other
          or is it the same?
               love and water
               love of water

sometimes a spirit rests in the darkness of the body

sometimes a spirit finds no rest before flight

some times find tests and marks of wear in the swirls

     of leaves by wind
     again leaves in autumn
     in a college town after
         one kind of loss
         one life's loss

life a series of asymmetries
and pronouns and gathas and twenties
and forties and works of light in the water
and out of the water

what did he see before in the worrisome light?
of a verb phrase or a nova or a no, sir,
other than the constant yes of
love
of the poems

when dreams were not and dreams were as air

we live in a time of hydration whether one is drinking water
in order to live or another jumps
from a boat in order to live where
boats and waters define and transcend
borders and honors
is there honor?
is there honor in a word a glance a light?

o love who places all where each is, no, that's
            too easy or maybe it all simply
            and decidedly should be easy and we just
consistently fuck it up with degrees of concern

contempt

                        or tempos

confused

and fused
            the foot is variable the word variable
            the line variable and when we set
                        it in stone we deny a force but when
                        we set it in type we augment a force on
                                    paper and in paper and
                                                remember that paper begins in
water

            as though grace
                        could save
                                    a language
                        in the dirt
            on the other
                        side of air

where a strange
      man turns forgetful
      not in a line or a foot or a variable motion
      in short, he wanders

      and the lettering of the wandering becomes
      a map of locations
      a map of tesselation
      a map, possibly of love, possibly other

he picks up a book again
      places stones again
            walks alone though not
            abandoned no matter
            what the child may imagine

the intention or the accident
      depends on the way the hand
            reaches through water always
past all accident

      penetrates or begins to penetrate
      again all the cracks   the crevices
of a world
      I will hate to leave
            an earthly paradise

or as much as one might have of one
the full and partial colors given
by one love
one woman through years
by those same and utterly strange waters

shared pictures of vessels
pictures of chairs
pictures of snow through car windows
pictures of windows and urban spaces
in New York and Paris
and home
home again where a blue deer finds us

but no not even the prospect of leaving and lead
me to bring this to a close
what does not close / is the will to open

open the will
open the door
open the flood gates
and we would if
only enough water
can be found

go about it the slow
    way, if you can
    whether it be money or
        water
        honey or
        mustard

the opposite of all is dearth
    a dearth of earth may be
    something to prescribe against
    something to prescribe in spite of
    something to describe in something
        less than meters or light years

he said "I am a poet! I am!" but where does that and a dollar
    land you, what land does it bear?

    not so dire
    as the sea remains
    is there in its profundity to admire
        and to warn
            sea, weeds, and as murmurous
    where murmurs are interruptions of heartbeats
        in the young and in the old
        in cases where kindness only begins
            the process

lucky to begin
     in the middle
          of an ocean
triple lucky with such love amid the blue
     they were kind to me there and in
          the midst of past dust bowls
     along route sixty-six and towns named
          Burns Flat and Dill City and Weatherford
     as though the weather might be forded
     as though we might afford the weather
          even if everything twists in the sky

     the leaves are very green, doctor
          my friend, my teacher
     my companion on a day early
          in a century of rising seas
          rising heat
          rising migration where migration
               only previews what
                    we all will know
the race is on and
     it looks like tumbleweeds
     through what once were
          meadows in which bare
               feet ran

one can not plan the poem, no
　　it happens in one's blinking moments
　　　　in one's mind and in the world
　　we imagine, but we only imagine what we make
　　have made and will make

　　　　may we have strength to keep the weeds at bay
　　　　many proclaim what leads us astray
　　　　and we can not pray
　　　　or go away
　　　　not today, no, not today

　　journey to love, perhaps
　　with everything open to the rain

　　　　remember that New York day
　　　　　　arriving at the conference
　　　　　　　　of "A" and "The" and "80 Flowers"
　　　　　　　　sopping wet from
　　　　　　　　the trains and the streets
　　　　　　removing socks and shoes to hang
　　　　　　　　　　and dry on racks

while we told stories of words and
    piled up stones of words
    left for lunch and returned
    left for air with Simon and
        did not return
    that kind of openness, to turn
        and return and not take
    much stock in stockpiling eloquence
    and addresses to rack up degrees
        of achievement

the words are best kept in poems
    most explosive there
    most wanting
    most saving

in that great storm,
    "Pitiful Lear," could you even
    then out-shout the room, out-
        shake the storm

go down, go down Persephone
  go down Kora
  go down Isis
  go down Jason
  go down Odysseus
      go down where the edge
      of the sea leads to some new turning
          some new slouching
          some new light, poem, love

I have been close to the mountaintop
and at the edge of the sea
and in your land of color scratched and brushed and
wept into paper

      inside that color we are one and not one
      inside the scratches we are two and not two
      inside the brush and the tears we sit
      hands in a soft circle
      eyes cast downward
      spines straight
          we may catch a light
  catch a word
      catch fire   catch air

catch a breath (which is a chance)

in the crater which also lay
      inside those colors and brushes we
         lay under a plethora of lights
   as though pinned against the bottom of a bowl
        where at the top the lights played
           with the universe, *sutil visitadora*
        cherry blossoms illumining
           the dark deep midnight blue sky
        you play with the light of the universe

we lay there together until over one lip of land
        sun rises again
        a dawn in the world we have yet
           to define or measure

in that cup
        and the cup is a poem
           we live with the light
           we live with the words
        of our own and others' making

what is the poem inside our breathing   breathing
 (repeat the word breathing slowly until
        no more utterance is possible
        no more breath remains)

so let's return there
     to the regular clerestories
          and the baltimore porches

     no, further back, Noel,
          when you swung a bat like an axe
          and laughed low and long, not loud
               but the laugh included us all
                    you, me, the water, the ducks
                    Ben, Justin, and the music,

     but it wasn't your heart in that power swing
          you were made for the poem, not
          the one written down but the one
          inside what was written down inside
          what will ever be written down

               so though you passed at the young
               age of 30, you really did not pass at all
               the song does not burn the song
               does not pass, the poem passes
               to the ages and I will help carry
               you and that swing and that laugh

into the next river
      into the still falling water
            the pushing falling deeply rolling waters

spring must have sprung
    as in my house I am
        dancing and
singing loudly to dylan's
    knockin' on heaven's door
        (but it's not too dark to see)
and writing
    this poem, which
        keeps all of those
    spinning things spinning
        drying the drenched
            shoes and socks
and searching for the saints, yes
        those saints, st rait and st range
        st and bp and all of the northern
        and southern lights with st francis
            among the daffodils

though here
    it's irises
    and roses
    I rises and
    I rose
    among the wildflowers
    on the other side
        not too dark
            but too bright
                at times
      to see
      the sun
      in the desert

            relents in the night and
            we sleep within the music

the desert music
    the insensate music
      where the dance begins
      and we attend
          bound into a whole
          by the poem that surrounds us

and that will be continued after the interlude of madrigals
                mad and regal, mindful and rugged, mass of
                right angles

        shake the flowers until
                the petals blue and white
                        fall to earth

but what goes on above?
        another young hawk after
            we had thought
the loss of the last one might
        be the end of the nest
            in our tree high
                    above the flower petals

            we have had hawks
            for a few years now
            their sad baby's cry for food
    and stern parental cries of warning

    the poem in the tree
    and the hawks in the tree

are the same thing
it is all the same
fabric if not the same weave
the big tent if not the same
gospel songs sung
no revival for there
has been no ebb tide
no loss

dive in or wade in or fall into the water
look up at the aleppo pine
know the colors of yellow green and blue
our eyesight measures the distance
the elements measure our eyes
and we know love is
to reason as eyes to mind
which gets us halfway there
the rest is act, use, playing the changes

as the past weekend we heard Mingus's Changes
    with piano trumpet saxophone drums and bass
        in a collective otherness
            not unison but
        excess and wandering in the same
                    time and tongue
                    weather and water

whereas once a wing and a word
    a wave and away
        blue and gray
        on a coast of dreams
        two coasts, more dreams
        among the seals in cold waters
            healed in cold waters
            knelt in cold waters
            or in a large hand lifted
            up with others, other
            peoples and rocks and
            plants and animals we
            share the hand, hear
            the bands, wrap around
            each other, dance into
            some new measure
                    some variable line

always columns growing on paper
like stacks of buildings or
            stacks of smoke in an autumn sky
            these we make to find home
            the home also the poem
            these we make to warm
                    together to warm
you of the bright and muted and ever changing colors
            to join words to what you bring, to bring words
            to what you join

                    words in columns words in waves
                    words in clouds words in communion
                    words in words in words as though
                    one might unfold the world there
                    and there and there as though
                    one could begin to be inside the word
                    inside the poem inside that love
                    incarnate, where carnate is a series
                    of seven letters seven columns of
                    lines arrangements of lines in
                    communion in folds in common

in folds and in fields one feels with a foot
            a path a presence a participle
                    presently without parrots

this (that word!) begins to sound
          like an interlude, and remember
                    the hedgehogs
(hardly hedgehogs)
                    form and from an
                              earlier pushing water
not the last pushing water
                    but sometime before the disease
sometime before the house became
                              a place for two
          now two others
off in the world (the wave, the enunciated word
                    funny to think, though
                    of being alone
                    on a small planet
                    where one thing connects
                              to another and
                              to all

          all the young dudes
          all the young falls
                    young winters
                    young springs
                    old summers

in a place losing its waters
      losing one's waters as
      losing one's mind
            getting too dark to see

oh that again / start it over
      kick it kick it kick it
      can't afford a ticket
            listen at the wall
            the home run wall
            the concert hall wall
            the border wall

if limits are what we are all inside
      what are borders or
            are there borders or

anyone might make
      a line
      a line that becomes a border
      but a line is just an infinity of points
            that might dissolve or must
            dissolve, maybe enough water
              will fall
            to dissolve the lines

dissolve as in
        gather and disperse
                contract and release
                a walk in the canyon where
                we see the dissolved rubies
                        the sand rubies
                        bring your face closer
                        your eyes closer
                                in the sand near
                                        the water
                                        not the last or least
                some comfort in the flow of wetness
                some gathering
                some hand holding it all

                like the hand of the dark woman
                        in the safeway grocery store
                                who asked me what I do
                and when I said
                        I am a poet she
                                reached into her bag
        to hand me a poem of her own
                because poetry is everywhere
                certainly in the carts and bags
                        of the dark women
                                in the grocery stores

who have heard the hawks
      and the horn sounds of psalms and loves
          supreme and echoing
in the wounds of those
      who return and in the wounds
          of those who do not return

do you see the water of the fountain
      flowing over the edge of the concrete
          in a thin sheet you can
push your hand through and feel
      what was there and what
          will be there in the next wet place
perhaps the last wet place
      to push through
          to walk in
to rest the poem
      where it might open
          to water air and light

the last of the pushing waters part 2

a wing

a wing

a wing

a wing

a wing

A WING

A WING

A WING

A WING

A WING

awning a wing

yawning among

humming along

a long along

after the wind

where do we go

afearing a friend might know

we left the ring on the tree

asking nothing of us
asking nothing of you
aching as an organ's vibrato
        or a heart's murmur

curing to an edge
coming to an end
unless a wing arrives
a way a word a rift
rift rift in time or
space where a cloud might
settle where settles a spark
a sparkling's wing as parking
        a ring
barking through the night
singing all days
arboreal
arbor arial
Ariel abounding
annie winging arial
a real free   a reel dance
among the trees upon the leaves
firefly or junebug song of light
song of flight or flight's answer
right there
on the tongue

taste a frightful answer
on the long tongue
taste an arial dancer
a fortunate one
for she tunes the colors
Iris she   maybe I rise   inside
the dream of light

(an aside) on the
side   anise as I die
to taste to know to
die
and then to taste
again
to dance until the
shoes are lost
to walk through the
remnant frost
of course that is
why the poem
remains
or came to visit ever
long ago
and decided to stay
and leave and stay

again the leaves
astray if when
one wing and
another spread
two on earth
surface
earth shifting shelf
moves
to free two selves
and
all the remaining
leaves fall
fall among
fall around (where
hedge-crickets sing

author acknowledgments

Many thanks to all who have helped with the work in this book. My
perceptive readers have been Joseph Lease, Andrew Levy, Hank
Lazer, and Will Alexander. As always, Cynthia E Miller has contrib-
uted not only her cover painting, but also ideas about the poetry
and design, and she suggested the title of the book. I owe a debt
to all of these, and more, in this book perhaps most significantly
to some forebears, particularly William Carlos Williams, Robert
Duncan, William Shakespeare, and Edmund Spenser. The writing of
the book was coterminal with the reading of Ludwig Wittgenstein's
Philosophical Investigations. My local colleagues who continue to
awe and inspire me include Tenney Nathanson, Steven Salmoni, and
Maryrose Larkin. Lynda Zwinger helped to inspire the poem "Lifting
Wing." David Weiss's brilliant work on the 19th Century poet Alfred
Tennyson helped to inspire my poem, "for now." Poetry is not a solo
art, but involves communities circling and interweaving other com-
munities, connections that sustain.

about the author

Charles Alexander is a maker. His primary area of making is poetry and essays, i.e. the art of words, but some people know him equally as a maker and publisher of books. His books include *Hopeful Buildings, arc of light / dark matter, Near or Random Acts, Certain Slants, Pushing Water* and *AT the Edge OF the Sea: Pushing Water II. Truro/Shift,* the third volume of *Pushing Water,* will be out in 2024. His poetry and prose have also been issued in more than a dozen chapbooks or fine press editions. He has taught at the University of Wisconsin-Madison, Naropa University, the Univ. of Arizona, Pima Community College, and the Univ. of Houston-Victoria. He is a former director of the Tucson Poetry Festival, helped to found and still serves on the board of POG (Poetry in Action), and was instrumental in the development of the Tucson Warehouse Arts District in the 1990s and early 2000s. He has participated in the TAMAAS Poetry Translation Project in Paris, France, and in the CAAP (Chinese American Association for Poetry and Poetics) conferences in China. His *Selected Poems,* translated by Chen Du, will be published in China. In 2021 he earned the CLMP award for lifetime achievement in literary publishing. He currently writes a column for American Book Review about poets/printers.

He is married to the artist Cynthia E. Miller.

about chax

Founded in 1984 in Tucson, Arizona, Chax has published more than
250 books in a variety of formats, including hand printed letterpress
books and chapbooks, hybrid chapbooks, book arts editions, and
trade paperback editions such as the book you are holding.
Chax also creates programs that engage students of literature and
of the arts of the book, through classes and workshops.
Chax presents several public events each year, including poetry
readings, artists' talks, and small symposia on topics of poetics,
the arts, and our social culture.

Your support of our projects as a reader, and as a benefactor, is much
appreciated.

You may find CHAX at *https://chax.org*

Albertina MT Pro has been used as the font throughout this book, with Gill Sans also used on the book's cover.

Designed at Chax Press

Printed at KC Book Manufacturing